TIME
THE
AVENGER

Time The

AVENGER

"Oh time! The beautifier of the dead, adorer or the ruin, comforter and only healer when the heart hath bled ... Time , the avenger!"

- Lord Byron

Poetry

by

Michelle Clemson

Dedicated to Sean-Mitchell

CONTENTS

A Haiku on Growing Pains

You learn who to trust
like you learn how to shave so
move your hand slowly.

How Do You Stop Them From Leaving?

He knows more words than me
more languages
as he languishes between ports
in lesser words I remind him to keep heart
and I'm dismissed in a different tongue.

A smile is a smile in any language
I want to save him
but he's too long at sea

He visits docks never staying long enough to get his
land legs

I want to save him, I smile, ignored
untying his ship – another land beckons
but not before
languishing at sea some more.

Mise En Garde

You cant boil your own blood
to warm another's heart
            another's corpse
no matter how big
your pot.

He's Not As Indescribable As I Once Thought...

His aura is a regimented navy blue
starched collar, scotch
on the rocks – at times.
His eyes a deep brown of fertile ground
from which the most gentle springs, when he smiles
Tempered, I observe with a pen
as he says
"She's writing about me again"

Eventualities

Douse yourself in me.
Light a match.
Know I am water.
Douse yourself in me.
I do not burn–
I erode.

Signature

I wrote her name as if it was mine.
I wrote her name
and filled a page.
Her name, my writing;
just how you'd like it. Her
name so rounded,
my writing so slanted.

I wrote her name as if it was mine
then lit the page
the pen
the book
the room
our home
me
us.

Verba Ex Humilis

It's in his eyes.
The earth spins too quick and
"*can you still it?*"
begged between gulps of distilled liquids
thoughts an ellipsis
imprisoned
It's in his eyes and he cant still it.

Verba Ex Humilis II

You can turn outlaw quick.
Society a fickle horse, due a bolt
to throw you to the floor
and trample upon you
as you foam like waves
crashing.. stilling.. ending
against rock
because there's only ever one ending for an outlaw.

Before You Meet Him...

The walls of your castle will come crashing down.
You'll run to the forest for shelter and the trees will burn to
ash.
You'll escape to the river, to replenish and
cleanse, to find drought and one solitary salmon
skeleton.
You will run to the depths of a cave, light a
fire, start to believe in tomorrow,
go to sleep smiling
wake to the bear eating your guts

But then you will heal, and your village will find you.
Your home will find you.

The Dream

There's us, you and I, in a house, not a home. Half
wooden shack, half floor-to-ceiling glass
too high off the ground for me to ever feel anything other than vertigo.
And there's a woman
patrolling our perimeter
I caught her looking at you with reservoir
eyes
 Do you know her?

"Write About What Scares You"

They go.
And they don't come back. Ever.

One by one. They go.
And they don't come back.

I look at who remains
what I fear is terrifying

and inevitable.

We all go
and never come back.
I wish I understood sooner
and went first.

Nabil

in temporary housing,
he waits,
on a sofa that is not his,
he waits
and we visit and he makes coffee
and tells us of home, his home,
the Basilia Ruins, the beauty,
the pictures of it in frames,
the pride in his eyes warming the room he does not own
and he waits
and since we've been visiting,
we've learned what
he waits for.

he's so over waiting, and is penalised
for
overstaying.

Did You See Me On TV Mum?

The dancing lights
of the sirens
compensated for
the stillness
of my
body.

From The Other Side (Of The Daily Mail)

"I sold everything I could get my hands on, including myself. You'll be pleased to hear I didn't once claim the dole, although your husbands' salaries still subsidised my living. Here, take a seat. Take a drink."

A Poem Voided But Days Later

Yesterday I noticed *him* on the horizon
and although there's no ignoring his shape I did
not allow myself to truly believe
he was back.

Today I wake to a stroke to my face,
a kiss to the neck, a hand on my waist
and there was no more ignoring
denying
I knew.

He is back
-the old you.
I melt into your touch and
feel
 a relief I left the gate
 open.

Weed

She is
dandelion seed
biding its time
to fly in the wind.

ID

Why am I still caterpillar
when they've all flown away? Or is
this my cocoon?
I have no wings, I know this
for I fell from a branch
trying to fly with them.

For Him

He's sick
of routine, the up in the morning and
bed before 10
the cold frost of his boss and early starts
packing his ego with his lunch
knowing its the pinnacle, summit,
peak, of any hope he had inside.
Dreams dying on the factory floor
under lights brighter than
the parts of his soul he exchanges for time and a half and
ask him the last time he saw a Saturday at home with his kids?
And he's sick
of the disconnection between his self worth and the love between his
wife and himself and the resentment that acts as a blanket stopping
them from
ever
truly
seeing
each
other
naked.
So sick, he needs a sick day
from work, from life, from the shopping lists and family trips that cost
more days at work than your soul can give.
He's sick and he doesnt talk to John about it either because John has
his own boss, his own wife, his own resentments, John, too, is sick,
He's sick and what can he do really?
Run away like his dad?
On the bus to work he dreams of an art studio, espressos and a love
without the duality of responsibility and resentment.
"Alright, John, Lad? Arsenal were shit again this weekend!"

All poetry and artwork written and produced by Michelle Clemson.
For enquiries please email <u>Mclemson1985@gmail.com</u>

Thank you for your Purchase.

Printed in Great Britain
by Amazon